Little RIDDLERS

Tiny Treasures

Edited By Davina Hopping

First published in Great Britain in 2018 by:

Young Writers
Remus House
Coltsfoot Drive
Peterborough
PE2 9BF
Telephone: 01733 890066
Website: www.youngwriters.co.uk

All Rights Reserved
Book Design by Ashley Janson
© Copyright Contributors 2017
SB ISBN 978-178896-138-7
Printed and bound in the UK by BookPrintingUK
Website: www.bookprintinguk.com
YB0347B

FOREWORD

Dear Reader,

Welcome to Little Riddlers - Tiny Treasures, are you ready to get your thinking caps on to puzzle your way through this wonderful collection?

Young Writers' Little Riddlers competition set out to encourage young writers to create their own riddles. Their answers could be whatever or whoever their imaginations desired; from people to places, animals to objects, food to seasons. Riddles are a great way to further the children's use of poetic expression, including onomatopoeia and similes; as well as encourage them to 'think outside the box' by providing clues without giving the answer away immediately.

All of us at Young Writers believe in the importance of inspiring young children to produce creative writing, including poetry, and we feel that seeing their own riddles in print will keep that creative spirit burning brightly and proudly.

We hope you enjoy riddling your way through this book as much as we enjoyed reading all the entries.

CONTENTS

Aghadrumsee Primary School, Aghadrumsee

Julie Anna Elliott (7)	1
Jacob Stephen Irwin (8)	2
Sam Forster (7)	3
Lee Wiggins (7)	4
Oliver Creighton-Clarke (7)	5
John McVitty (8)	6
Jodie Robinson (6)	7
Ben Forster (6)	8
Ryan Morrison (7)	9
Abbie Coulson (6)	10
Jordan Nelson (8)	11
Ryan McVitty (7)	12
Sophie Morrison (6)	13

Ashlea Primary And Nursery School, Tullyally

Shay Quinn (6)	14
Emily McKegan	15
Rebekah McClay (6)	16
Shanice Donnell (7)	17
Sophia Gardner (6)	18
Grace Smallwoods (4)	19

Barmby Moor CE Primary School, Barmby Moor

Tilly Ava Lucas (7)	20
Madalin Farrow (6)	21
Kara Thompson (7)	22
Sam Dawson (6)	23
Rose Beatrice Pape (6)	24
Sophie De Klein (6)	25
Kayleigh Hubbard	26
Max John Hubbard (6)	27

Beattock Primary School, Beattock

Blake Evan McEwan (7)	28
Tegan McClelland (6)	29
Mason Thomas Crooke (5)	30
Evan William McIntyre (7)	31
Ellie-Mae Bentley (4)	32
James Gardinor (7)	33
Leah Wilson (6)	34
Lucy Davidson (6)	35
Austin Robert Clarkson (7)	36
Tia Morgan Crooke (6)	37
Kiera Sprott (7)	38
Kelvin Anderson (7)	39
Ellie Davidson (4)	40

Bournmoor Primary School, Bournmoor

India Ryan (5)	41
Freddie Todd (5)	42
Amelie Baughan (5)	43

Gaelscoil Na Móna, Belfast

Oahran Shannon, Ayesha, Katie, Pádraig Bradley & Michael	44
Nathan Kearns, Jessica, Aimee & Ruby Darcan	45

Amy White-Fox (7), Cara, Pól-Og, Clodagh, Keelan & Patrick Martin Conlon	46
Ryley Sean Irvine (7), Rhys, Chloe, Anthony & Hannah	47

Gurney Pease Primary School, Darlington

Mithura Pathmaselvan (7)	48
Lyla-Rose Jeanes (6)	49
Riley Buxton (6)	50
Aeryn Taylor (6)	51

Headlands CE (VC) Junior, Infant And Nursery School, Liversedge

Esme Bradley (6)	52
Daisy Wigley (6)	53
Tommy Sagar (6)	54
Lydia Rose Hutton (6)	55
Isabella Parkin (6)	56
Eva Pickard (6)	57
Lois Claughton (6)	58
Abdurrahman Abbas (6)	59
Rayansh Nag	60
Molly Margrave	61
Jacob Lee Jackson (6)	62
Isla Stocks (6)	63
Layla Rushforth	64
Daisy Broomhead	65
Evie Rhodes (6)	66
Eva Wild (5)	67
Thomas George Brackenbury (6)	68
Kora Hepworth (5)	69
Lola Hutton (5)	70
Ashton- Lee Taylor (5)	71

La Moye School, St Brelade

Ruby Boschat (6)	72
Elliott Hewlett (5)	73
Year 1T Class	74
Ffion Beth Davies (5)	75

Kacper Piechota (5), Alanna Flambard & Olivia Winiarz	76
Theo Depledge (6)	77
Year 1D Class (5)	78
Xanthe Gibson (5)	79
Joel Kenny (5)	80
Isaac McAllister (5)	81
Ruairidh Joe Daly (5)	82
Jessica Le Miere (5)	83
Beatrice Searle (5)	84
Caleb Byrne (6)	85
Gabriel Kaminski (5), Olivier Kudelski & Hala Parsley	86
Lilliana Osmand (5)	87
Henri Fallaize (5)	88
George Fitz-Thomas (5)	89

Mayfair International Academy, Estepona

Victoria Gudkova (6)	90
Alberto Andrades Marin (6)	91

Nada International School, Al Hasa

Ali Haytharn (6)	92
Ahmad Mohammad Khattab (6)	93
Alishba Irfan Nawaz (6)	94

New Farm Primary School, Kilmarnock

Paula Beth O'Neill (7)	95
Lyle Storrie (7)	96
Paige Millar (7)	97
Nathan Gilmour (7)	98
Aaron James Galloway (7)	99
Olivia Sim (7)	100
Sophie Ann Begg (6)	101
Andrew McCallum (7)	102
Teigan Helen Weir (7)	103
Aiden Robert Morrison (7)	104
Malcolm Paterson (6)	105
Reese Steele (7)	106

Jennifer Mair (6) 107
Jamie Allan (7) 108
Jack James Connelly (6) 109

Newtownabbey Independent Christian School, Glengormley

Micah David Brown (5) 110
Heidi Clarke (5) 111

Saint Patrick's Primary School, Shotts

Abigail Cierniewska (7) 112
Sarah Franciszka Ludorf-Deans (7) 113
Paige A E Brown (7) 114
Mia Aldous (7) 115
Michael Coulter (7) 116
Taylor Healy (7) 117
Leon Joseph (6) 118
Jake Watters (7) 119
Anna Mullen (6) 120
Ryan Laidlaw (7) 121
Josh McLean (7) 122
Sean Kelly (6) 123
Aara Sweeney (7) 124
Shanna E Duffy (6) 125
Caleb Janczak (7) 126
Joshua Leckie (7) 127
Aimee Leek (7) 128

St Blasius CE Primary Academy, Shanklin

Hollie Kenny (6) 129
Lena Brodowska (6) 130
Charlie Luckman (7) 131
Kelsey Smith (7) 132
Alesha Paige Ganderton (7) 133
Kaitlin Hilson (6) 134
Mitchell Reeves (6) 135
Dexter Staples (6) 136
Jenny Sheppard (6) 137

Daniel Dopierala (6) 138
Megan McCluskey (6) 139
Adele Sanders (6) 140
Tyler Jay Bolton (7) 141

St Brigid's Primary School, Ballymoney

Grace Mullaghan (6) 142
Kyle Smith (7) 143
Caolan Kelly (7) 144
Alfie Dunlop (6) 145
Ethan Guiney (6) 146
Ciaran Kirgan (6) 147
Charlie O'Brien (7) 148
Ollie Kirgan McClenaghan (6) 149
Mylie McAleese (7) 150
Olly J Mc Laughlin (7) 151
Nicole Kowalewska (7) 152

St Mary's CE Primary School, Slough

Aayan Ahmed (6) 153
Yash Chawla (6) 154

St Mary's Primary School, Annalong

Darcy Mc Donagh (6) 155
Erin-Louise Hammond (6) 156
Kyla Rea (6) 157

St Teresa's Primary School, Lurgan

Hollyanne Kearney (7) 158
Aoife News (8) 159
Shannon Maria Mallon (7) 160

Woodlands Primary School, Paisley

Peyton Burns (7) 161
Amy Rose Morton (7) 162

Keela Clark (7)	163
Aimee Rankine (7)	164
Jaxon Matthew (7)	165
Robyn Matthews (6)	166
Callum Blacklock (7)	167
Charley McEwan (7)	168
Logan Paton (7)	169
Alex Maslanka (7)	170
Nairn Dunlop (7)	171
Kayla Tweedie (7)	172

THE POEMS

Midnight Flight

I am as soft as a pony
I have eyesight as good as a fox's
I live in trees as tall as houses
I have a beak as small as your nose
I soar like a kite
I have claws that are as prickly as a hedgehog
I have wings as long as a bookshelf
I eat insects as small as a little button
I say tu-whit tu-whoo as loud as a whistle
I am as brown as a horse
I am nocturnal.
What am I?

Answer: An owl.

Julie Anna Elliott (7)
Aghadrumsee Primary School, Aghadrumsee

What Am I?

I can be as a big as a tree
I can be on fire like a fire twister
I can roll like a ball
I am built like a house
I can be as small as a mouse
I can climb like a monkey
I can fly like a dragon
I can be as long as a lorry
I can be as dangerous as a lion
I can be as loud as an elephant
I can be as fast as a cheetah.
What am I?

Answer: A robot.

Jacob Stephen Irwin (8)
Aghadrumsee Primary School, Aghadrumsee

Winter White

I am as cold as ice
I am wet as water
I don't move like ice
I melt into water
You build stuff with me
I come in flakes from the sky
I make a *slash* sound
I am as white as a piece of paper
I am as white as the wool on a sheep.
What am I?

Answer: Snow.

Sam Forster (7)
Aghadrumsee Primary School, Aghadrumsee

Space

I am as quiet as a mouse
I am far away
I am as still as a statue
There is only one of me
I am as hot as an oven
I sizzle like a frying pan
You can't touch me
I am as bright as a light
I don't speak, hear or see.
What am I?

Answer: *The sun.*

Lee Wiggins (7)
Aghadrumsee Primary School, Aghadrumsee

Jumping High

I am as fast as a cheetah
I have good hearing
I am as soft as a cushion
I have sharp claws
I always land on my feet
I can climb trees
I can come in stripes or patches
Dogs can chase me
I miaow and purr
I eat mice and food.
What am I?

Answer: A cat.

Oliver Creighton-Clarke (7)
Aghadrumsee Primary School, Aghadrumsee

Farm Machine

I am as strong as a lorry
I am as powerful as a digger
I have black lineage
My noise is *brum, brum*
I am as noisy as an elephant
I am as big as a gate
What am I?

Answer: A tractor.

John McVitty (8)
Aghadrumsee Primary School, Aghadrumsee

Springtime

I am as fluffy as an owl
I can jump
I say *baa*
I am cuddly
I eat hay
I drink water
I can be fidgety sometimes
I am sometimes noisy
I am very small
I am cute.
What am I?

Answer: A lamb.

Jodie Robinson (6)
Aghadrumsee Primary School, Aghadrumsee

Farm Creature

I am heavy
I am big
I am strange
I am furry
I can jump
I am fat
I am as smelly as a rubbish dump
I like grass
I have not very many teeth
I am as noisy as a monkey
I make milk.
What am I?

Answer: A cow.

Ben Forster (6)
Aghadrumsee Primary School, Aghadrumsee

Farm Animal

It feeds calves
It eats meal feed
It is brown, black or white
It lives on a farm
It is smelly
It says 'moo'
It makes milk
It has hooves
It is as soft as a cat
What is it?

Answer: A cow.

Ryan Morrison (7)
Aghadrumsee Primary School, Aghadrumsee

What Am I?

I have good eyesight
I have a bushy tail
I have fur
I have baby cubs
I like to eat chicken
I have sharp teeth
I catch prey
I am as wild as a cheetah.
What am I?

Answer: A fox.

Abbie Coulson (6)
Aghadrumsee Primary School, Aghadrumsee

What Am I?

My sting can kill
I buzz like bees
I fly like a bird
I am yellow and black
I live in hot places
I am as scary as a dinosaur
I have a queen
What am I?

Answer: A hornet.

Jordan Nelson (8)
Aghadrumsee Primary School, Aghadrumsee

What Am I?

I am black and white
I can jump high
I have a tail
I can run fast
I am a pet
I drink milk and water
I miaow
I purr
I am as soft as a pillow.
What am I?

Answer: A cat.

Ryan McVitty (7)
Aghadrumsee Primary School, Aghadrumsee

What Am I?

I am yellow and have spots
I am as tall as a house
I have a long neck
I eat leaves, *munch, crunch!*
I live in Africa.
What am I?

Answer: A giraffe.

Sophie Morrison (6)
Aghadrumsee Primary School, Aghadrumsee

What Am I?

I'm fast like the wind
I play with a ball
I shout when I get a cramp
When I play with the ball I shout
When I play I wear shorts and a T-shirt
People come to watch me.
What am I?

Answer: A footballer.

Shay Quinn (6)
Ashlea Primary And Nursery School, Tullyally

What Am I?

I am fluffy
You can snuggle me
You can play with me
I am as quiet as a mouse
I am as fluffy as a blanket.
What am I?

Answer: A teddy bear.

Emily McKegan
Ashlea Primary And Nursery School, Tullyally

What Are They?

They are big
They are stripy
They eat meat
Sometimes you see them in a zoo.
What are they?

Answer: Tigers.

Rebekah McClay (6)
Ashlea Primary And Nursery School, Tullyally

Living In The Zoo

They climb trees
They hang from trees
They are brown
They are funny.
What are they?

Answer: Monkeys.

Shanice Donnell (7)
Ashlea Primary And Nursery School, Tullyally

What Am I?

I make flowers grow
The leaves on the trees are green
People go walking.
What am I?

Answer: Spring.

Sophia Gardner (6)
Ashlea Primary And Nursery School, Tullyally

What Are They?

They eat grass
They are fluffy
They walk quite loudly.
What are they?

Answer: Sheep.

Grace Smallwoods (4)
Ashlea Primary And Nursery School, Tullyally

Whizz Wallop

I'm only meant to come out once a year.
I can really, really hurt your ears.
Do not touch me with your hands
As I am still very hot when I land.
I do not work well in the light.
I look much better during the night.
I sound like popcorn in the sky.
Watch me twinkle as I go by.
What am I?

Answer: Fireworks.

Tilly Ava Lucas (7)
Barmby Moor CE Primary School, Barmby Moor

Foxey Roxey Goes For A Walk

I have a fluffy coat, all soft and shiny.
My nose is wet and soft like a sponge.
I can sit and beg on one leg.
If I am good you give me treats.
My tongue is wet and slippery.
Tickle my belly and I won't eat your wellies.
What am I?

Answer: A dog.

Madalin Farrow (6)
Barmby Moor CE Primary School, Barmby Moor

Scrummy

Chocolate, vanilla, strawberry,
Fruit and lemon too,
Weddings, birthdays, Christmas,
It's really up to you.
As big as an elephant,
As small as a crumb,
I don't mind as long as it goes in my tum.
What am I?

Answer: A cake.

Kara Thompson (7)
Barmby Moor CE Primary School, Barmby Moor

Funny Honey

I am only small
But I have a big sting.
I have six legs but I mostly use my wings.
I live in a hive and fly high in the sky.
I can be seen in the flowers.
Collecting nectar is one of my superpowers.
What am I?

Answer: A bee.

Sam Dawson (6)
Barmby Moor CE Primary School, Barmby Moor

What Am I?

He is very funny.
He has four feet.
He is black and white.
He likes to eat meat.
He loves stealing socks from the basket and giving them to you.
He is my very best friend.
Who is he?

Answer: My dog, Sam.

Rose Beatrice Pape (6)
Barmby Moor CE Primary School, Barmby Moor

Hot Frog

Eggs are used to make me
Milk is used to make me
I am golden brown
I taste so nice
I do pop up
I am not a frog
I smell like pork
I come from Yorkshire
I am very hot.
What am I?

Answer: Toad in the hole.

Sophie De Klein (6)
Barmby Moor CE Primary School, Barmby Moor

Warm Hugs

He melts in summer into a big wet puddle
His nose is a carrot
He wears my daddy's scarf
Because he is as cold as ice.
What is he?

Answer: A snowman.

Kayleigh Hubbard
Barmby Moor CE Primary School, Barmby Moor

The Jungle Roar

In the jungle he roars like a lion
He is orange and black
He eats meat
He has four legs
so he can jump as high as a frog.
What is he?

Answer: A tiger.

Max John Hubbard (6)
Barmby Moor CE Primary School, Barmby Moor

The Spots

I am extremely spotty like a cow.
I am black, white and really fuzzy.
I have sharp claws
But I only use them when I'm annoyed.
I have long curly ears
That go over my eyes when I am scared.
When I need the toilet I go outside.
I have four white legs
That I use to walk with.
What am I?

Answer: A Dalmatian.

Blake Evan McEwan (7)
Beattock Primary School, Beattock

What Am I?

I am glass with sand inside me.
I can roll around like a cylinder.
Time runs through me.
My sand can be sparkly.
My sand will never see the sea.
I time things.
I don't have hands
And I don't have a face.
What am I?

Answer: A timer.

Tegan McClelland (6)
Beattock Primary School, Beattock

Scary

I scare things.
I have a bucket for my face
And a stick for my body.
I live in a field in some mud.
I have long, long arms.
I wear clothes.
I never move.
What am I?

Answer: A scarecrow.

Mason Thomas Crooke (5)
Beattock Primary School, Beattock

The Armour

I live in a castle but I am not a lord
I have armour and also a sword
I have a shield
I save princesses
I always go on adventures
I slay dragons.
What am I?

Answer: A knight.

Evan William McIntyre (7)
Beattock Primary School, Beattock

Woof

I give cuddles and play
I have fluffy fur and a tail
I have special baby food
I visit the vet with my owner
I get lots of pats from my owner.
What am I?

Answer: A puppy.

Ellie-Mae Bentley (4)
Beattock Primary School, Beattock

Skinny Thing

I am long and thin
I can be different colours
I make marks on paper
I can be sharp and blunt
You use me for writing
I live in a case.
What am I?

Answer: A pencil.

James Gardinor (7)
Beattock Primary School, Beattock

Squeak And Squeak

I am really, really thin
I have a thin and long tail
I have big ears
I have a really pink nose
I have whiskers
I have little, tiny toes.
What am I?

Answer: A mouse.

Leah Wilson (6)
Beattock Primary School, Beattock

The Game Machine

I have a mouse but no cage
I am a square
I have a screen
You can play on me
I have hard parts and soft parts
I have lots of buttons.
What am I?

Answer: A computer.

Lucy Davidson (6)
Beattock Primary School, Beattock

The Snap

I can snap angrily
I can swim fast
I don't swim in the sea
I am a scary predator
I don't eat people
I have a long head.
What am I?

Answer: An alligator.

Austin Robert Clarkson (7)
Beattock Primary School, Beattock

The Spots

I am black and white
I am spotty
I go outside to play
I am good at sniffing
I am good at hide-and-seek
I don't say moo.
What am I?

Answer: A Dalmation.

Tia Morgan Crooke (6)
Beattock Primary School, Beattock

Running Wild

I am really strong
I am massive
I am so, so hairy
You can sit on me
I can take you places
I wear clumpy shoes.
What am I?

Answer: A horse.

Kiera Sprott (7)
Beattock Primary School, Beattock

The Naughty Friend

I am fluffy
I have sharp, pointy teeth
I sleep outside
I love digging big holes
I get in trouble.
What am I?

Answer: A dog.

Kelvin Anderson (7)
Beattock Primary School, Beattock

Night-Time

I feel soft and fluffy
I am cuddly
I give lots of kisses
I sleep lots
I have whiskers.
What am I?

Answer: A kitten.

Ellie Davidson (4)
Beattock Primary School, Beattock

The Wheels

I have three wheels and two handles.
You have to push on the floor to
make me go.
I come in different colours.
You have to push the brake to stop.
I am really fun.
What am I?

Answer: A scooter.

India Ryan (5)
Bournmoor Primary School, Bournmoor

Zoom!

I come in all colours
I come in different sizes
You can ride in me on the road
I have a boot to put things in
I can go fast and slow
You can drive me.
What am I?

Answer: A car.

Freddie Todd (5)
Bournmoor Primary School, Bournmoor

Colourful!

I grow from a seed
I need soil and water
I am colourful
I need sun
I am pretty.
What am I?

Answer: A flower.

Amelie Baughan (5)
Bournmoor Primary School, Bournmoor

The Beautiful Night

I have big eyes with small feet.
I flash before your eyes,
gliding through the sky.
I sleep all day and at night I hunt my prey.
I am as beautiful as the night stars
As I fly over your cars.
I fly deep in the dark, cold woods
Trying to find some good food.
I'm as brown as a bear
and faster than a hare.
What am I?

Answer: An owl.

Oahran Shannon, Ayesha, Katie, Pádraig Bradley & Michael
Gaelscoil Na Móna, Belfast

The Charging Beast

I have a lot of keys but they don't jingle.
I'm busy all day and I always have time to play.
Your memories are safe with me and they always will be.
I can be as quiet as a mouse and I live in your house.
Don't forget to plug me into the socket before bed.
I shut down or you will be wearing a frown.
What am I?

Answer: A laptop.

Nathan Kearns, Jessica, Aimee & Ruby Darcan
Gaelscoil Na Móna, Belfast

Dead Man Walking

I am as white as a ghost
When I appear you jump out of your seat
I walk with no shoes and a *creak*
No flesh on my bones
My skin has peeled like an orange
My eyes have popped out like a piñata
I am dead, heartless and soulless.
What am I?

Answer: A skeleton.

Amy White-Fox (7), Cara, Pól-Og, Clodagh, Keelan & Patrick Martin Conlon
Gaelscoil Na Móna, Belfast

Jolly Good Holiday

On my face sits a snowy mountain.
I need a big black belt to hold my tummy in.
I find my cookies and milk yummy.
My friends are small and funny
And they work fast like a bunny.
I give out gifts based on my very long list.
I'm jolly and fat and wear a bright red hat!
Who am I?

Answer: Santa.

Ryley Sean Irvine (7), Rhys, Chloe, Anthony & Hannah
Gaelscoil Na Móna, Belfast

A Moment Of Magic

I can be found in the bright green field
Eating my favourite food.
I like to trot.
When I trot along, I go clip-clop
Around the street because I use my hooves.
I feel smooth like a light feather
Floating gently to the ground.
I have soft, white hair
That covers my whole body.
I have got four legs.
I have a sparkly, pointy horn
Which elves use for magic.
What animal am I?

Answer: A unicorn.

Mithura Pathmaselvan (7)
Gurney Pease Primary School, Darlington

The Mysterious Creature

I feel smooth and fluffy
so people snuggle me.
I can be found in a pet shop
and in the streets.
I can make tiny, minute sounds
but I can also scratch.
I have a small nose and it is fluffy.
I am a scratcher, a snuggler and a cutie.
I have a special chip
which lets me in the door
so that cats can't get me.
What am I?

Answer: A cat.

Lyla-Rose Jeanes (6)
Gurney Pease Primary School, Darlington

The Paleontologist

I feel like a stone and I'm heavy.
I have a long tail
And sharp teeth to tear enemies!
I sound like an over the top lion.
I can be found as a fossil under the ground
Because I'm from the olden days.
I look like a mini version of a T-rex.
I'm a cousin of the T-rex but a bit smaller.
What am I?

Answer: A seeker.

Riley Buxton (6)
Gurney Pease Primary School, Darlington

Fabulous Flutterer

I feel soft and delicate so people can't touch me.
I can be found in the white clouds high up in the sky.
I am the baby of the sky.
I sound like a shooting star whizzing around.
I have wings and I am colourful.
I lived in a cocoon which can be found in a tree.
What am I?

Answer: A butterfly.

Aeryn Taylor (6)
Gurney Pease Primary School, Darlington

Slow But Fast

I only play when the sun is out
I walk quite slow without a doubt
But you better watch out or I'm out of sight
My favourite food is dandelion flowers
I eat them for over an hour
When I eat I'm like a lawnmower
I have four legs and a house on my back
When I am dirty I make a track
I sleep under lights
All through the dark cold nights
I sleep until morning then I yawn.
What am I?

Answer: A tortoise.

Esme Bradley (6)
Headlands CE (VC) Junior, Infant And Nursery School, Liversedge

What Am I?

I roam around the jungle all day
Avoiding the poachers in my way.
In the world I can run free
With my hairy mane for all to see.
I run so fast to catch my prey
When the sun goes down I love to lay.
I am fierce with a mighty roar,
Watch I don't scratch you with my paw.
I don't want to be captured
And put in a zoo,
I want to be free, just like you.
What am I?

Answer: A lion.

Daisy Wigley (6)
Headlands CE (VC) Junior, Infant And Nursery School, Liversedge

In The Sky

I am green and sometimes mean.
I can fly in the sky.
I have a broom and a smelly room.
I have a wart on my nose
and wear black clothes.
I have a cat that is black and a pointy hat.
You might have heard me cackle,
When I ate Hansel and Gretel.
Who am I?

Answer: A witch.

Tommy Sagar (6)
Headlands CE (VC) Junior, Infant And Nursery School, Liversedge

Fierce Cat

I'm as fast as the wind.
I growl like a bear.
I live in the jungle
but you can see me in a zoo.
My tongue is red like a strawberry.
I have eyes as black as a bin bag.
My teeth are as sharp as a big knife.
I am black and orange like a pencil.
What am I?

Answer: A tiger.

Lydia Rose Hutton (6)
Headlands CE (VC) Junior, Infant And Nursery School, Liversedge

What Am I?

I can be red, pink, white or yellow.
I smell so nice that ladies can wear me.
My food helps the bees make honey.
You can pick me
And wear me in your hair.
My body is green
But watch out I might hurt!
I can be given as a gift.
What am I?

Answer: A rose.

Isabella Parkin (6)
Headlands CE (VC) Junior, Infant And Nursery School, Liversedge

Time For A Riddle?

I have a face but no eyes
I have hands but can't clap
I will tell you something without talking
I am exactly the same just twice a day
I can run but can't walk
The sound I make rhymes with my name.
What am I?

Answer: A clock.

Eva Pickard (6)
Headlands CE (VC) Junior, Infant And Nursery School, Liversedge

Fantastic Beast

Killed by knights, gives princesses frights
Horns on head, kill you dead
Fairy tale, swishy tails
Red and black, scaly back
Breathing fire, flying higher and higher
In my story, fierce and gory.
What am I?

Answer: A dragon.

Lois Claughton (6)
Headlands CE (VC) Junior, Infant And Nursery School, Liversedge

What Am I?

Roll your dice again and again...
You might get six
Play on your own or with friends
Go up some ladders
You win when you reach one hundred
You go up on some numbers.
What am I?

Answer: Snakes and ladders.

Abdurrahman Abbas (6)
Headlands CE (VC) Junior, Infant And Nursery School, Liversedge

What Am I?

I have more than two legs and two eyes.
I eat bugs and flies.
I crawl around the room
And don't make a sound.
If I bite a man
He will turn into a hero like Superman.
What am I?

Answer: A spider.

Rayansh Nag
Headlands CE (VC) Junior, Infant And Nursery School, Liversedge

My Fiery Friend

I like to blast fire out
I can be mean and fearless
I like to fly high as the sky
My scales are shiny
I like to battle with knights
I have sharp teeth to snap things up.
What am I?

Answer: A dragon.

Molly Margrave
Headlands CE (VC) Junior, Infant And Nursery School, Liversedge

Zigzag Beast

I have black stripes
I eat grass
I don't like lions
I make a sound like this - *nayayayaya*
I am also wild
I sleep under a tree
I live in the zoo.
What am I?

Answer: A zebra.

Jacob Lee Jackson (6)
Headlands CE (VC) Junior, Infant And Nursery School, Liversedge

Big But Small

I run and run till it's no more fun.
I am black and white
so I am not very bright.
I have long large legs and muddy feet
with big ears to hear my treats.
What am I?

Answer: A dog.

Isla Stocks (6)
Headlands CE (VC) Junior, Infant And Nursery School, Liversedge

What Am I?

I have a pointy horn
I'm a magical creature
I have a rainbow mane
You can find me in a story book
I can gallop like a horse
I live in an enchanted forest.
What am I?

Answer: A unicorn.

Layla Rushforth
Headlands CE (VC) Junior, Infant And Nursery School, Liversedge

What Am I?

I swim in the sea
I have scales on my tail
I can breathe underwater and on land
I sometimes sit on rocks and talk to fishes.
What am I?

Answer: A mermaid.

Daisy Broomhead
Headlands CE (VC) Junior, Infant And Nursery School, Liversedge

What Am I?

You might see me on the street after it rains
If you look in me you can see your reflection
Some kids like to splash in me.
What am I?

Answer: A puddle.

Evie Rhodes (6)
Headlands CE (VC) Junior, Infant And Nursery School, Liversedge

Do I Play Fair?

Africa I'm at
I'm not a pet cat
Yellow and black
Spots on my back
I eat meat
Fast on my feet.
What am I?

Answer: A cheetah.

Eva Wild (5)
Headlands CE (VC) Junior, Infant And Nursery School, Liversedge

Who Am I?

Good footballer
Best hugger
Dog walker
Bedtime story reader
Washing up master
Hard worker
Funny dancer.
Who am I?

Answer: Daddy.

Thomas George Brackenbury (6)
Headlands CE (VC) Junior, Infant And Nursery School, Liversedge

What Am I?

Leaf power
I can be really tall or sometimes quite small
I can have many leaves or none at all
What am I?

Answer: A tree.

Kora Hepworth (5)
Headlands CE (VC) Junior, Infant And Nursery School, Liversedge

What Am I?

I have big ears
I have a long trunk
I have big tusks
I live in Africa.
What am I?

Answer: An elephant.

Lola Hutton (5)
Headlands CE (VC) Junior, Infant And Nursery School, Liversedge

What Am I?

I am yellow
I am long
I could make you really strong.
What am I?

Answer: A banana.

Ashton- Lee Taylor (5)
Headlands CE (VC) Junior, Infant And Nursery School, Liversedge

Fab Fast Food

I look like a yummy snack
I sound like sizzling sausages
You find me on a plate
I have a bottom and a top
I am best served with toppings and ketchup
I am a fast food treat.
What am I?

Answer: A burger.

Ruby Boschat (6)
La Moye School, St Brelade

Prehistoric Predator

I have big eyes
and a long tail.
I can roar.
I am extinct.
You find me in the jungle.
I have two big feet.
I have two short arms.
What am I?

Answer: A dinosaur.

Elliott Hewlett (5)
La Moye School, St Brelade

A Fruit Bowl Snack

I look like a round beach ball.
I sound crunchy like leaves.
You find me on a tree in the orchard.
I have pips in the middle.
I am red or green.
I feel smooth.
What am I?

Answer: An apple.

Year 1T Class
La Moye School, St Brelade

A Tall Helper

I look like a tower.
I sound like whispering voices.
You find me in the forest
I have roots.
I am a house.
I feel soft at the top
And hard at the bottom.
What am I?

Answer: A tree.

Ffion Beth Davies (5)
La Moye School, St Brelade

A Slithering Surprise

I am quiet.
I am long.
I have scales.
I live in the jungle.
I eat lots of animals.
I hiss.
I shed my skin.
What am I?

Answer: A snake.

Kacper Piechota (5), Alanna Flambard & Olivia Winiarz
La Moye School, St Brelade

Pirates' Delight

I look like the sparkly sun
I sound like clinking cups
You find me in a chest buried underground
I have secrets to share
I feel hard and warm.
What am I?

Answer: Treasure.

Theo Depledge (6)
La Moye School, St Brelade

A Cheeky Friend

I am cheeky
I sound like laughter
You find me in the jungle
I have big ears and a long tail
I am brown and love bananas
I feel soft.
What am I?

Answer: A monkey.

Year 1D Class (5)
La Moye School, St Brelade

A Gentle Giant

I look like a ladder
I sound like a washing machine
You find me in Africa
I am a super leaf eater
I feel soft like a blanket.
What am I?

Answer: A giraffe.

Xanthe Gibson (5)
La Moye School, St Brelade

A Bumpy Desert

I look like a mountain
I sound like a spitting child
You find me in the desert
I have a furry tongue
I am very smelly.
What am I?

Answer: A camel.

Joel Kenny (5)
La Moye School, St Brelade

Prehistoric Predator

I have sharp teeth
I stomp when I walk
I am extinct
You find me in the jungle
I am green
I have two small arms.
What am I?

Answer: A dinosaur.

Isaac McAllister (5)
La Moye School, St Brelade

A Black Creature

I look like a bird
I sound like a baby crying
You find me in the woods
I have big wings
I am a fruit eater
I feel soft.
What am I?

Answer: A bat.

Ruairidh Joe Daly (5)
La Moye School, St Brelade

A Healthy Treat

I look like a flower
I sound silent
You find me in a box
I have a coat of hair
I am red
I am best served as jam.
What am I?

Answer: A raspberry.

Jessica Le Miere (5)
La Moye School, St Brelade

Sea Explorer

I look like a hairy monster
I sound like *arg!*
You find me at sea
I am a treasure hunter
I have a parrot.
What am I?

Answer: A pirate.

Beatrice Searle (5)
La Moye School, St Brelade

Grass Eater

I look like a cow
I sound like *neigh*
You find me in a field
I have a long tail
I am good at galloping.
What am I?

Answer: A horse.

Caleb Byrne (6)
La Moye School, St Brelade

King Of The Jungle

I have a hairy mane
My mane is orange
You find me in the jungle
I hunt for my food
I have four paws
I roar.
What am I?

Answer: A lion.

Gabriel Kaminski (5), Olivier Kudelski & Hala Parsley
La Moye School, St Brelade

A Mythical Beauty

I have rainbow hair
I have a horn on my head
I can gallop
I eat apples
I can neigh
I look like a horse.
What am I?

Answer: A unicorn.

Lilliana Osmand (5)
La Moye School, St Brelade

What Am I?

I look like a bird
I sound like a wolf
You find me in the night
I have no shadow
I am spooky.
What am I?

Answer: A ghost.

Henri Fallaize (5)
La Moye School, St Brelade

Night Hunter

I look like a bird
I sound like a baby crying
You find me in the woods
I have black wings.
What am I?

Answer: A bat.

George Fitz-Thomas (5)
La Moye School, St Brelade

Rare Creature

I'm like a horse, that's how it seems
I'm like a fish that hardly swims
I can be red or blue or brown
That all depends if sun is down
I like to drift and eat seaweed.
So tell me, what am I indeed?

Answer: A seahorse.

Victoria Gudkova (6)
Mayfair International Academy, Estepona

What Animal Am I?

I lay eggs
I have the skin of a mole
I have the tail of a beaver
I have the beak of a duck
I have the legs of an otter
I have the teeth of a rat.
What am I?

Answer: A platypus.

Alberto Andrades Marin (6)
Mayfair International Academy, Estepona

Naughty Little Animal

I am green.
In the pond I can be seen.
I have friends,
Ducks and leaves with big tears.
I am jumping up and down
Looking for insects all around.
I can't fly.
What am I?

Answer: A frog.

Ali Haytharn (6)
Nada International School, Al Hasa

The Monster

I have sharp teeth
I am long and big
I have a long neck
I have a long tail
I have fire inside
I have a horn
What am I?

Answer: A dragon.

Ahmad Mohammad Khattab (6)
Nada International School, Al Hasa

Fire Maker

Open up my tummy,
Hit me on my side,
And you will get
A lot of light
And a big fire.
What am I?

Answer: A matchbox.

Alishba Irfan Nawaz (6)
Nada International School, Al Hasa

The Swimming Creature

I am a type of dinner or lunch
I have two fins and a tail
I like cold water
People like to taste me
Sharks like to eat me
You can catch me on a rod
I blub a lot of the time.
What am I?

Answer: A fish.

Paula Beth O'Neill (7)
New Farm Primary School, Kilmarnock

The Cube In The Corner

I have thousands of channels
I have music channels too
You can turn me off and on
You can lift me to your new home
You can sit me on a unit
People own me
You watch me.
What am I?

Answer: A television.

Lyle Storrie (7)
New Farm Primary School, Kilmarnock

The Best Pet

I am soft and furry
I have a waggy tail
My nose is as wet as rain
People take me for a walk
I eat my food from a bowl
Chasing cats is my favourite hobby
I bark a lot.
What am I?

Answer: A dog.

Paige Millar (7)
New Farm Primary School, Kilmarnock

The Nut Cruncher

I am small
I climb up trees
I run fast
I don't like dogs
I like nuts but not coconuts
I have a bushy tail like a dog
You sometimes see me in the forest.
What am I?

Answer: A squirrel.

Nathan Gilmour (7)
New Farm Primary School, Kilmarnock

The Very Small Creature

My body is long
Under my body are loads of legs
I live outside
I don't like wood
I like leaves
My skin changes colour
I change into a butterfly.
What am I?

Answer: A caterpillar.

Aaron James Galloway (7)
New Farm Primary School, Kilmarnock

Yummy Dessert

You can eat me
I am not a vegetable
I hate knives
I have icing
I may be fat
You can put decorations on me
I have candles
I am round like a clock.
What am I?

Answer: A birthday cake.

Olivia Sim (7)
New Farm Primary School, Kilmarnock

Tiny Tot

I am very cute
My face is small
I crawl a lot
I love milk
I live in a house
People like to cuddle me
I am smiley
I like to sleep a lot
I like to cry.
Who am I?

Answer: A baby.

Sophie Ann Begg (6)
New Farm Primary School, Kilmarnock

Weeble Wobble

People like to eat me
I am red, orange or green
I don't like the heat
I like cold things
I wobble like a penguin
I live in the fridge.
What am I?

Answer: A jelly.

Andrew McCallum (7)
New Farm Primary School, Kilmarnock

Hot Home

I move on four legs
I live in the desert
I have lumps on my back
People like to ride on me
I am furry
I am called the ship of the desert.
What am I?

Answer: A camel.

Teigan Helen Weir (7)
New Farm Primary School, Kilmarnock

Somewhere Comfy To Sit

I have four legs
I am comfy
I want to be lifted through the kitchen
People push me in and pull me out
I live in any room in the house.
What am I?

Answer: A chair.

Aiden Robert Morrison (7)
New Farm Primary School, Kilmarnock

My Favourite Pet

I am furry
I can run faster than a dog
I like to play with toys
Fish are what I like to eat
I sleep in a basket
When I am happy I purr.
What am I?

Answer: A cat.

Malcolm Paterson (6)
New Farm Primary School, Kilmarnock

Bzzz Bzzz

I fly a lot
You see me in trees
I don't like birds
You might see me in your house
I'm black and yellow
I go *buzz buzz*.
What am I?

Answer: A bee.

Reese Steele (7)
New Farm Primary School, Kilmarnock

The Barker

I have a wet nose
I run like a cat
I live in a house
I like to lick people
I am a cat's enemy
I like to chase cats and bark.
What am I?

Answer: A dog.

Jennifer Mair (6)
New Farm Primary School, Kilmarnock

Ice Cold

I am black and white
I waddle about like a bird
I am cold
I am not a pet
I can be wet
I like to dive
My feet are orange.
What am I?

Answer: A penguin.

Jamie Allan (7)
New Farm Primary School, Kilmarnock

Cold Snack

I am tasty
I am cold
You can eat me
I am flavoured
I am coloured
I can melt.
What am I?

Answer: An ice lolly.

Jack James Connelly (6)
New Farm Primary School, Kilmarnock

Ding Ding Dong

Ding, ding
Bing, ding, dong
Can you hear me?
I'm red and black
As fast as a stripy tiger
Cling, cling
I have wheels
My handlebars are like cylinders.
What am I?

Answer: A bicycle.

Micah David Brown (5)
Newtownabbey Independent Christian School, Glengormley

A Place To Sit

I can sit on it
It has legs
It is comfy
It lives in a school
When you swing on it, it goes *bang, bang*
It has four legs like a dog.
What is it?

Answer: A chair.

Heidi Clarke (5)
Newtownabbey Independent Christian School, Glengormley

Nature Love

I make my gran cake
but I'm not a baker.
I pick flowers
but I'm not a florist.
I am a brave girl
but I'm not a superhero.
I'm very happy
but I'm not a princess.
I never talk to strangers.
Who am I?

Answer: *Little Red Riding Hood.*

Abigail Cierniewska (7)
Saint Patrick's Primary School, Shotts

The Cutie Pie Orangy

I'm quite little and I like to sleep
I hug my mum a lot
I am so orange
I look like the sun shinning
I growl when I'm angry
I love fluffiness
I love my name, it's cute, very cute
I am so fuzzy wuzzy.
What am I?

Answer: A baby fox.

Sarah Franciszka Ludorf-Deans (7)
Saint Patrick's Primary School, Shotts

Slipiddy Dip

I am a fish lover.
I am a type of bird
but I can't fly.
I like to swim
And catch the fish on my own.
I sometimes slip and slide.
I am the cutest thing you can find.
What am I?

Answer: A penguin.

Paige A E Brown (7)
Saint Patrick's Primary School, Shotts

Nature Lover

I am a princess but I am not Belle
I am friendly but I am not Cinderella
I am generous but I am not Aurora
I love rabbits but I am not Rapunzel
I have black hair but I am not Moana.
Who am I?

Answer: Snow White.

Mia Aldous (7)
Saint Patrick's Primary School, Shotts

A Hero

I can sometimes wear chain gear
And I have a sword.
I can ride a horse but I'm not a jockey.
I've been known to fight dragons.
I can be a king or a prince.
Who am I?

Answer: A knight.

Michael Coulter (7)
Saint Patrick's Primary School, Shotts

The Fluffy Mystery

I eat carrots but I don't eat stew
I hop about but I'm not a kangaroo
I'm very fluffy but I'm not a cat
I'm as cute as a button and that's that.
What am I?

Answer: A bunny.

Taylor Healy (7)
Saint Patrick's Primary School, Shotts

The Vegetable

When you buy me
you skin me and eat me.
After you eat me
you throw me away.
I'm as sweet as sugar
and I go *pop!*
but I'm not popcorn.
What am I?

Answer: Sweetcorn.

Leon Joseph (6)
Saint Patrick's Primary School, Shotts

The Hunter

I am orange
But I'm not an orange.
I have a bushy tail
But I'm not a squirrel.
I am as sneaky as a thief
But I only steal food.
What am I?

Answer: A fox.

Jake Watters (7)
Saint Patrick's Primary School, Shotts

The Sparkly Press

I have a wand
but I'm not a witch.
I am a girl.
I am small
and sometimes sparkly.
I go *twinkle, twinkle*.
I am as cute as a robin.
What am I?

Answer: A fairy.

Anna Mullen (6)
Saint Patrick's Primary School, Shotts

A Special Superhero

I shoot webs but I am not a spider
I am a superhero but not Batman
I use webs to climb very high buildings
I talk but no one knows my name.
Who am I?

Answer: Spider-Man.

Ryan Laidlaw (7)
Saint Patrick's Primary School, Shotts

An Alien

I am very friendly
but I'm not a pet.
I am very special
but money can't buy me.
I can do most things
but I'm not a robot.
What am I?

Answer: A human being.

Josh McLean (7)
Saint Patrick's Primary School, Shotts

A Wobbly Little Fella

I fall out a lot
but I am not hair.
I wobble
but I am not toes.
I am sharp
but I am not glass.
I am white
but I am not a cloud.
What am I?

Answer: A tooth.

Sean Kelly (6)
Saint Patrick's Primary School, Shotts

A Magical Myth

I am a magical horse.
I have rainbow hair.
I have a horn
but I am not a bull.
I love to fly
but I am not a bird.
What am I?

Answer: A unicorn.

Aara Sweeney (7)
Saint Patrick's Primary School, Shotts

The Colourful Flyer

I can be colourful and I can fly
I have wings and I bob next to flowers
I make no noise
I come out when it is hot.
What am I?

Answer: A butterfly.

Shanna E Duffy (6)
Saint Patrick's Primary School, Shotts

A Jungle Creature

I am fierce, but I am not alone
I am a fast runner but I'm not a cheetah
I have stripes but I'm not a zebra.
What am I?

Answer: A tiger.

Caleb Janczak (7)
Saint Patrick's Primary School, Shotts

The Blood Sucker

I have a cape
but I am not Superman.
I have fangs
but I am not a wolf.
I can fly
but I am not a bat.
What am I?

Answer: Count Dracula.

Joshua Leckie (7)
Saint Patrick's Primary School, Shotts

A Pet

I love to sniff
I love to play
I love to sleep every day
I'm as cute as a button
I'm very chunky.
What am I?

Answer: A pug.

Aimee Leek (7)
Saint Patrick's Primary School, Shotts

Can You Guess?

It is as soft as a cloud
It is as fluffy as cotton wool
It is as cute as a rabbit
It likes to eat biscuits
It has a flap to go outside
It purrs when you stroke it
It likes to catch mice
It is a type of animal
Sometimes it is fidgety
Some are orange and stripy
When it's born sometime it says miaow first.
What is it?

Answer: A kitten.

Hollie Kenny (6)
St Blasius CE Primary Academy, Shanklin

10 Clues, Can You Guess?

It is fluffy like a cloud
It is cute like a rose
It has cute legs like a wolf
It likes dog food
It hates cats
It is not as little as a mouse
It has eyes as green as a frog
It has a waggy tail
It has brown and white fur
It goes *woof, woof.*
What is it?

Answer: A puppy.

Lena Brodowska (6)
St Blasius CE Primary Academy, Shanklin

What Is It?

It can be red, green or mouldy
It can be crunchy
You can cook it in a pie
You can have it in your lunchbox
You can eat it because it is healthy for you
You can play with it and roll it
And you can use it to dunk at Halloween.
What is it?

Answer: An apple.

Charlie Luckman (7)
St Blasius CE Primary Academy, Shanklin

Can You Guess?

It feels smooth and hairy
It likes bananas
It makes this *ooh, aa, aa* sound
It climbs in trees and swings high
It likes being hot
It can be big or small.
What is it?

Answer: A monkey.

Kelsey Smith (7)
St Blasius CE Primary Academy, Shanklin

It Can Be...

It can be cute
It can be nice
It can be scratchy
It can be lovely
It can be kind
It can be adorable
It can miaow
It can lick
It can be as fluffy as a rabbit.
What is it?

Answer: A kitten.

Alesha Paige Ganderton (7)
St Blasius CE Primary Academy, Shanklin

Who Am I?

I'm good at jumping
I love carrots
My tail is white and fluffy
I munch and crunch my lunch
I'm as soft as a pillow
You can see me in the spring.
What am I?

Answer: A baby rabbit.

Kaitlin Hilson (6)
St Blasius CE Primary Academy, Shanklin

Vrmmm Vrmmm

It has two handles like a pram
It is as heavy as a car
It has a chain like a necklace
It has an engine like a mower
It has a seat like a saddled horse
What is it?

Answer: A motorbike.

Mitchell Reeves (6)
St Blasius CE Primary Academy, Shanklin

A Jumpy Riddle

It likes flies
It has four legs
It jumps very high
It is an amphibian
It likes water
It ribbits
Sometimes it will bite you.
What is it?

Answer: A frog.

Dexter Staples (6)
St Blasius CE Primary Academy, Shanklin

What Are They?

They are cuter than a rabbit.
They say a quiet miaow.
They have a flap to go out.
They can be good and sometimes bad.
They sometimes are fidgety
but always cuddly.
What are they?

Answer: Kittens.

Jenny Sheppard (6)
St Blasius CE Primary Academy, Shanklin

What Am I?

I'm good at swimming and running fast
I wag my tail when I'm happy
I bark and growl
I'm as fast as a footballer
I'm an excellent pet!
What am I?

Answer: An excellent dog.

Daniel Dopierala (6)
St Blasius CE Primary Academy, Shanklin

What Am I?

I have teeth and claws
My skin is bumpy
I sway and splash my tail in the water
I snap and clap my jaws together
I'm as scary as a monster.
What am I?

Answer: A crafty crocodile.

Megan McCluskey (6)
St Blasius CE Primary Academy, Shanklin

Carnivore

It is orange, stripy and black
It has cubs when it is pregnant
It can roar when it is angry
It eats meat.
What is it?

Answer: A tiger.

Adele Sanders (6)
St Blasius CE Primary Academy, Shanklin

Toasted And Tasty

It is nice to eat
It is tasty
It is yummy as a sandwich
It is a great lunch
It is delicious
It goes crunch.
What is it?

Answer: A burger.

Tyler Jay Bolton (7)
St Blasius CE Primary Academy, Shanklin

Who Is She?

I would like to play with her
She is the best
She is so fun
She is so cool
She is so pretty
She's got lots of bright bows.
Who is she?

Answer: Jojo

Grace Mullaghan (6)
St Brigid's Primary School, Ballymoney

What Am I?

I live on the ocean floor
I live two hundred metres deep
I'm very big
I'm not nocturnal
I'm the size of a house.
What am I?

Answer: A whale.

Kyle Smith (7)
St Brigid's Primary School, Ballymoney

What Am I?

I am as pink as a pig
I sizzle in a pan
I am tasty
I come in lots of sizes
I am in a fry-up
You find me in a shop.
What am I?

Answer: Bacon.

Caolan Kelly (7)
St Brigid's Primary School, Ballymoney

Riddles

It is fast
It is brown
It has four legs
It is big
It has shoes
It is really noisy
It has a tail.
What is it?

Answer: A horse.

Alfie Dunlop (6)
St Brigid's Primary School, Ballymoney

What Is It?

It goes slowly
You think it is real
It is invisible
It is like it plays hide-and-seek
It is scary.
What is it?

Answer: A ghost.

Ethan Guiney (6)
St Brigid's Primary School, Ballymoney

What Am I?

I have an engine
I am big
I float
I go fast
I go on top of the water
I have a steering wheel.
What am I?

Answer: A boat.

Ciaran Kirgan (6)
St Brigid's Primary School, Ballymoney

What Am I?

You can sit on me
I have wheels that spin around
I have a chain at the bottom.
Can you guess what I am?

Answer: A bicycle.

Charlie O'Brien (7)
St Brigid's Primary School, Ballymoney

It's Coming

I am red and dark
I have horns
My eyes are as dark as the night
I am scary.
Who am I?

Answer: *The Devil.*

Ollie Kirgan McClenaghan (6)
St Brigid's Primary School, Ballymoney

Fairy Tale

It has a dress
It has a crown
It has a tall house, curly hair and a gown.
What is it?

Answer: A princess.

Mylie McAleese (7)
St Brigid's Primary School, Ballymoney

Snap

I make a *snap* noise
I live in the swamp
I am green
I have very sharp teeth.
What am I?

Answer: A crocodile.

Olly J Mc Laughlin (7)
St Brigid's Primary School, Ballymoney

What Am I?

I am white
I have bones
I scare you
I can kill you.
What am I?

Answer: A skeleton.

Nicole Kowalewska (7)
St Brigid's Primary School, Ballymoney

A Sky Power

I come in different colours and styles.
I come in different sizes, big and small.
You can ride me for miles and miles.
When I appear,
You may hear me whistle, *shhh, grrrr*.
I have very clean and comfy seats.
I have six wheels and wings.
I am made from metal.
You can see me in the sky
But you cannot touch me.
What am I?

Answer: An aeroplane.

Aayan Ahmed (6)
St Mary's CE Primary School, Slough

Nasty Little Things

I make you sneeze
I am in the breeze
I am smaller than a dot
I can never be caught
I am very scary
Stay away from me, as I am a nasty thing
I can only be killed by medicine.
What am I?

Answer: A virus.

Yash Chawla (6)
St Mary's CE Primary School, Slough

Snap Trap

I am long and lie still as a log
but my big teeth you will not snog.
I remember the dinosaurs
now fishermen beat me with oars.
My skin is rough like bark
so you don't confuse me with a shark.
They made my mum into handbags
and my dad into shoes and gladrags.
When the water around me is lapping
it is then my teeth will come snapping.
What am I?

Answer: A crocodile.

Darcy Mc Donagh (6)
St Mary's Primary School, Annalong

The Golden Ticket

Chocolate factory
Oompa loompa
Charlie's friend
Sweet-eater
Golden ticket-winner
Mad as a hatter
Funny as a joke.
Who is it?

Answer: Willy Wonka.

Erin-Louise Hammond (6)
St Mary's Primary School, Annalong

Friends For Life

They love you
Care about you
Go out with you
Have fun with you
Tickle and laugh together.
What are they?

Answer: A family.

Kyla Rea (6)
St Mary's Primary School, Annalong

Up And Down

I go up and I go down
And yet I never move around.
Take me in ones, twos or threes
Just be careful to mind your knees.
Under me there can be space
To store your coats, your boots or case.
My electric cousins live in the store
Travel on them and you can buy more.
Climb me at night to reach your bed
Take your time, you sleepy head.
What am I?

Answer: Stairs.

Hollyanne Kearney (7)
St Teresa's Primary School, Lurgan

Thanks A Bunch

Most people say I've got a beautiful scent.
I wouldn't survive inside a dark tent.
Bees *buzz* round to visit me
And then make honey for your tea.
I come in different shapes and sizes.
You might find me in competition prizes.
I have been known to share girls' names.
I do like water, I don't like flames.
What am I?

Answer: A flower.

Aoife News (8)
St Teresa's Primary School, Lurgan

My Auntie's Best Friend

My auntie is called Mable,
She keeps it in a stable.
She has another one called May
And she feeds it hay.
She says it's a doddle
To put on a saddle.
Using a little whip
She gives them a clip.
And off they go for a trot
And that's your lot.
What am I?

Answer: A horse.

Shannon Maria Mallon (7)
St Teresa's Primary School, Lurgan

In The Jungle

I am a juicy, raw meat eater.
I hate the soaking wet rain.
I have very thick skin.
I live in very sunny Asia.
I love the shiny, bright sun.
I drink out of lakes.
I have orange fur with black stripes.
I would be second in a race
against a cheetah.
What am I?

Answer: A tiger.

Peyton Burns (7)
Woodlands Primary School, Paisley

In The Jungle

I am really fast
I live in Africa and jungles
I have sharp claws
I really hate the rain
My patterns on my fur are black spots
I eat fish
I love the sun so much
I am always hot
I am the fastest animal on Earth.
What am I?

Answer: A cheetah.

Amy Rose Morton (7)
Woodlands Primary School, Paisley

Around The Park

I have really fluffy fur
I like my belly rubbed
I don't like rain or fire
I have sharp, tiny claws
I like my food called chicken and barbecue
I drink cold, fresh water
I like to go for long walks with my owners.
What am I?

Answer: A dog.

Keela Clark (7)
Woodlands Primary School, Paisley

In Around The House

I am super fluffy
I've got really sharp teeth
I am so friendly and purry
I am cuddly and like rubbing against legs
I am often sleeping
I've got sharp claws
I drink white, creamy milk
I am a greedy meat eater.
What am I?

Answer: A cat.

Aimee Rankine (7)
Woodlands Primary School, Paisley

In The Sand

I like to eat nice juicy food
I am the star on a telly advert
I can be found in a popular safari park
I am a small, cute animal
I have sold lots of house and car insurance
You can get a Star Wars one or me.
What am I?

Answer: A meerkat.

Jaxon Matthew (7)
Woodlands Primary School, Paisley

Big Bird

I have silky, soft feathers
I am a bright, beautiful pink
I stretch my big, long wings
I eat wet, slippery fish
I have long, yellow legs
I have a sharp, yellow beak
I am a big, tall bird.
What am I?

Answer: A flamingo.

Robyn Matthews (6)
Woodlands Primary School, Paisley

My Favourite Place

It is a giant, big place
It has lots of big hotels
It has lots of busy trams
It has a long, sandy beach
It has lots of exciting, scary rides
It has a huge tower with a glass floor.
Where am I?

Answer: Blackpool.

Callum Blacklock (7)
Woodlands Primary School, Paisley

Lucky Thing

I am soft and cuddly
I am black and furry
I love getting petted from my owner
I sometimes lie and play with you
I always drink white, creamy milk
I hate the cold and wet.
What am I?

Answer: A black cat.

Charley McEwan (7)
Woodlands Primary School, Paisley

In The Jungle

It starred in a children's film
It loves to climb trees
It is soft to touch
It has a fluffy tail
People keep it as a pet
Its friend's name is Alvin.
What is it?

Answer: A chipmunk.

Logan Paton (7)
Woodlands Primary School, Paisley

Hanging Around

I have a long, furry tail
I can balance using my tail
I am very silly
I am super smart
I eat juicy fruits and crunch vegetables
I like to swing on tall trees.
What am I?

Answer: A monkey.

Alex Maslanka (7)
Woodlands Primary School, Paisley

On The African Plains

I can eat juicy green leaves
I can see a long distance away
I have a thick neck
I have two big tusks
I have huge flappy ears
I have a very useful trunk.
What am I?

Answer: An elephant.

Nairn Dunlop (7)
Woodlands Primary School, Paisley

In China

I am big and fat
I am black and white
I come from China
I have long, sharp claws
I am a type of mammal
I eat bamboo.
What am I?

Answer: A panda.

Kayla Tweedie (7)
Woodlands Primary School, Paisley

Est.1991

YOUNG WRITERS INFORMATION

We hope you have enjoyed reading this book – and that you will continue to in the coming years.

If you're a young writer who enjoys reading and creative writing, or the parent of an enthusiastic poet or story writer, do visit our website **www.youngwriters.co.uk**. Here you will find free competitions, workshops and games, as well as recommended reads, a poetry glossary and our blog.

If you would like to order further copies of this book, or any of our other titles, then please give us a call or visit **www.youngwriters.co.uk**.

Young Writers
Remus House
Coltsfoot Drive
Peterborough
PE2 9BF
(01733) 890066
info@youngwriters.co.uk